BASEBALL LEGENDS AND THEIR LIFE LESSONS

UNLOCKING CHARACTER THROUGH THE JOURNEYS OF BASEBALL ICONS

INSPIRATIONAL STORIES FOR KIDS

EMMA HOPE

STORIES THAT INSPIRE

Inspiring the Future, One Story at a Time

https://storiesthatinspire.com/baseball-legends-free-gift

Dear Baseball Enthusiast,

If you've been inspired by the stories of Babe Ruth, Jackie Robinson, Lou Gehrig, and other icons in "Baseball Legends and Their Life Lessons," we have a special opportunity for you to deepen that inspiration.

📖 FREE COMPANION JOURNAL

Dive deeper into your personal growth with our specially designed journal. Reflect on your goals, find your inner courage, and discover what truly drives you. Each chapter of the journal corresponds with a legend from the book, offering guided prompts to help you draw lessons from their lives and apply them to your own.

• Challenge yourself like Babe Ruth: Set ambitious goals and strategize ways to overcome obstacles.

• Embrace bravery with Jackie Robinson: Reflect on your experiences with adversity and how you've faced them.

• Find resilience in the story of Lou Gehrig: Consider what makes you persevere in tough times.

🏆 ONLINE QUIZ: TEST YOUR KNOWLEDGE

Think you know everything about these baseball legends? Put your knowledge to the test with our exclusive online quiz. It's a fun and interactive way to revisit the key moments and achievements of these iconic players.

• Chapters aligned with the book: Each quiz section relates directly to a chapter in the book.

• Engaging questions: Challenge your memory and understanding of each legend's story.

INTRODUCTION

Baseball is about warm summer days, sitting in the stands eating a hot dog, drinking soda, and watching an epic battle play out on the baseball diamond. It's you hoping this time your team comes out on top. And to add that cherry on top – you hope to see at least one player hit a home run!

On the field of any Major League Baseball (MLB) game, you'll be watching world-class players who have tested themselves over and over again. Players who have met problems along the way and faced them head-on with courage and strength, both mental and physical. Sometimes they won and sometimes they didn't. But when they lost, they never gave up. They got back up and tried again, and maybe even again and again, until they finally were successful. They kept at it until they made it to the big leagues and became professional baseball players.

Most who tried fell by the wayside. They didn't have that special something inside that kept them going. The ones you're watching play out on the baseball diamond on that sunny summer afternoon are the ones who had that certain set of character traits that got them to the top.

What can we learn from those players? How can we use those lessons in our own lives?

That's what this book is all about!

Baseball is a unique sport for creating inspirational legends. It's a team sport, so it needs players to be able to work together. They must cooperate. They need to understand each other's strengths and weaknesses. They need to communicate with each other. They must learn to set goals together and then work and train to meet them as a team.

But then, in many ways, baseball is an individual sport. For example, each player has a batting average. This is the number of hits they've had divided by the number of times they've batted. For example, if they've batted 500 times and out of those 500 times they've got 100 hits, their batting average would be .200. This has nothing to do with the team. It's all about the individual player. A committed player will train in the batting cage to improve their batting average. That takes self-discipline. Not everyone has that.

The same goes for defensive play. A pitcher is judged by how he keeps batters from getting hits. He's all alone up there on the pitcher's mound. An outfielder has no help from his team when the high flying ball is heading towards him. Whether it lands in his glove or misses and bounces to the ground, it's all up to the individual player. Baseball is a sport that allows for individual excellence.

That combination of having the skills to work together with others on a team and the courage to face big challenges all alone creates baseball legends who can inspire us. In this book, you'll meet some of the biggest heroes of the game and learn what sets them apart from others. Hopefully, what you learn from the lives of these inspirational baseball legends will help you to build your character and live a life that can inspire the people around you.

Now let's meet some of these baseball legends!

CHAPTER 1
BABE RUTH

"I never forgot where I came from. Every dirty-faced kid I see is another useful citizen."
— Babe Ruth

INTRODUCTION

BABE RUTH'S love for children was well known. No matter where he was, he had time to stop and give an autograph to a child. There are many stories about sick children in the hospital getting secret visits from Babe, visits with no reporters or photographers, just Babe there to brighten a sick kid's day and sign a baseball for him. Leon Fichman was a child actor in a film where Babe appeared. He never forgot the bigger-than-life baseball star. "He was the nicest man I ever met. He was so nice to all of us kids for those two weeks. I'll never forget a minute of it."

Babe's heart had a soft spot for kids because he knew how

hard life could be for them: it had been hard for him when he was a child. Babe Ruth went on to be rich, famous, and beloved, but he started life quite a bit differently.

EARLY LIFE

Babe was born George Herman Ruth on February 6, 1895. His parents were both from poor, working-class, German families living in Baltimore, Maryland. Babe's parents did all sorts of work to keep the family going. They worked so hard that in his autobiography, *The Babe Ruth Story*, Babe says he didn't really know his parents at all. No one was paying him any attention, so he ran the streets, skipping school and causing problems in the neighborhood. Later, when he spoke about his early life, he was honest about the sort of childhood he'd had and the kind of child he had been.

"I was a bad kid. I say that without pride but with a feeling that it is better to say it. Because I live with one great hope in mind: to help kids who now stand where I stood as a boy. If what I have to say here helps even one of them avoid some of my own mistakes, or take heart from such triumphs as I have had, this book will serve its purpose."

ST MARY'S AND FATHER MATTHIAS

His parents needed to do something about his bad behavior. When Babe was seven years old, they decided to send him to St. Mary's Industrial School for Boys. On June 14, 1902, Babe was sent away to that boarding school. He rarely saw his parents again. The school was an orphanage and a reformatory, a place to reform or change bad boys into good ones. In Babe's records from the school, the reason for his being admitted was that he was "incorrigible."

He received an education at St. Mary's and learned some useful skills, but most importantly, it was at St. Mary's he learned how to play baseball. That introduction to baseball was thanks to one of the teachers at the school, the Prefect of Discipline, Brother Matthias Boutilier, who would become Babe's life-long role model and mentor.

Brother Matthias was 6 feet 6 inches tall and weighed 250 pounds; Babe described him as "all muscle." Later, when Babe spoke about Brother Matthias, he said that he could have been successful at anything he chose to do with his life, but he chose the church.

It was Brother Matthias who taught Babe how to hit a baseball. "I never forget the first time I saw him hit a ball... the ball would carry 350 feet. A tremendous knock in those days. I would watch bug-eyed," Babe said.

Babe played nearly all of the positions on the school baseball team, and he played them using a right-handed baseball glove even though he was left-handed. Though he was good everywhere, he soon became the team's star pitcher.

Brother Matthias could see Babe's talent and wanted to make sure other people saw it too. The school invited Jack Dunn, the owner of the then Minor League team the Baltimore Orioles, to come and see Babe play. Dunn watched Babe play for less than an hour and in February 1914 offered the then 19-year-old his first professional baseball contract.

Because of St Mary's and Brother Matthias, Babe became a life-long Catholic. His whole life, he made donations to the school and made personal appearances to help in their fundraising. In 1926, when Babe had become a famous baseball player, he bought Brother Matthias a Cadillac for $5000, a huge amount of money at the time. Later, it was wrecked beyond repair in a car accident, and Babe bought his mentor another one to replace it.

START OF HIS PROFESSIONAL CAREER

Because Babe was only 19 years old when he began as a professional player, Jack Dunn had to become his legal guardian. When he arrived for training with his new team, the other players called him "Jack Dunn's babe." Soon it became just "Babe," and that remained his name from then on.

Despite being a new player, Babe had a cocky, arrogant way about him that the other players didn't like. His first time in the batting cage, they wanted to teach him a lesson by sawing all of his bats in half. It didn't trouble Babe, though. His was a big, bold, confident, sometimes rough personality, and he wasn't going to let himself be pushed into being someone he was not. He was who he was, and no one was going to get in his way because he had a dream: he was going to be the best baseball player the world had ever seen.

In 1914, though he was in the Minor League Orioles, he played five games in the Major League with the Boston Red Sox. His first game as a Major League player was on July 11, 1914. By 1915, he was a permanent member of the Red Sox, playing as a pitcher. He would be with the Boston Red Sox for six seasons. In 1915, Babe pitched nine shut-out games in a row, meaning not a single player got a hit off any of his pitches. This was a record-setting feat for a left-handed pitcher. Babe was on his way to greatness!

With the Red Sox, he was an excellent pitcher, but as a

pitcher, he didn't play every game. The team had other good pitchers who sometimes played instead of Babe. If he was not playing, he wouldn't get a chance to bat, and Babe didn't like this. He was becoming known as a player who hit home runs, not such a common thing at this time in the game of baseball. In 1919, Babe's last season with the Red Sox, there were only 447 home runs hit in the entire Major League that season. Babe made 29 of them. He wanted to be batting every game, and though he liked pitching and was good at it, he knew he might have to give it up.

In 1920, Babe was traded to the New York Yankees. There he changed a few things. He became an outfielder in any game that he was not pitching so that he would be at the plate every game. That sacrifice made a big difference. He was about to break all the records for batting in the Major League.

CURSE OF THE BAMBINO

When Babe was with the Red Sox, they won five of the first sixteen World Series. When he transferred to the Yankees, the Red Sox didn't win another World Series until 2004—86 years later. "Bambino" was another one of Babe's nicknames, and some called that long period of the Red Sox's losing the Curse of the Bambino.

While the Red Sox struggled, the fortunes of the Yankees headed the other way. When Babe arrived, they'd never won the American League pennant or been part of any World Series. Once he was on their team, that all changed. With Babe on the team, they won seven American League pennants and four World Series.

Babe became the first baseball superstar and celebrity. People talked about him; they recognized him on the street. The stadiums were full whenever he played. Fans wanted to see Babe hit a home run, and he never wanted to let them down. Sportswriter Glen Stout said, "A Babe Ruth home run was an event in itself, one that meant anything was possible."

With the Yankees, he set record after record. In 1920, Babe hit 54 home runs for the season. The player in second place for home runs that year hit 19. On July 18, 1921, Babe hit the 139th home run of his career, breaking the record of 138. For the rest of his career, until he retired in 1935, after playing 22 seasons of professional baseball, he toppled record after record.

BABE'S LEGACY

When Babe retired, he held 56 Major League records. He was in the first group of five players inducted into the Baseball Hall of Fame in 1936. He died on August 16, 1948. Two days later, his funeral was held at St. Patrick's Cathedral in New York. 100,000 people lined the streets to bid their beloved Babe Ruth his last farewell.

Babe Ruth was a poor, uneducated boy with no family connections. All he had was talent and an overwhelming ambition to be successful, but that was enough. In *The Big Bam*, a biography about Babe Ruth written by Leigh Montville, he calls Babe "the patron saint of American possibility," which seems just about right.

DISCUSSION QUESTIONS

1. Do you think Babe's parents made the right decision to send him to St Mary's? Why, or why not?

2. Although Babe was an excellent pitcher and was very proud of that, he gave it up and became an outfielder so that he could bat every game. What do you think about this decision?

3. Leigh Montville called Babe Ruth "the patron saint of American possibility." What does that mean?

FREE BONUS CONTENT

CHAPTER 2
JACKIE ROBINSON

"A life is not important except in the impact it has on other lives."
– Jackie Robinson

INTRODUCTION

IN THE EARLY days of baseball, a few African Americans were allowed to play on teams with white players, but by 1898, the color bar that stopped all blacks from playing professional baseball with whites was firmly enforced – that was until Jackie Robinson arrived.

On April 15, 1947, Jackie Robinson walked onto the baseball field playing in Major League Baseball (MLB) for the Brooklyn Dodgers, the first African American to have done so since 1898. It was not an easy door to force open, but when he did it, he kept it open for other African American players to follow, and Major League Baseball was never the same again.

EARLY LIFE

Jackie Robinson was born on January 31, 1919, the youngest child of Mallie and Jerry Robinson. His parents were both from sharecropper families in Georgia. The Robinsons moved to Pasadena, California, and raised their children there. Jackie's older brothers could see the youngest in the family was on the wrong path, hanging out with a bad crowd, and encouraged him to apply to John Muir Technical High School and concentrate on sports. One of his older brothers, Mack Robinson, excelled at track and field and went on to win a silver medal in the 200-meter race at the Berlin Olympics in 1936.

At John Muir, Jackie showed what an extraordinary athlete he was. Most students were lucky to play varsity in one sport; Jackie played varsity in four: football, basketball, track and field, and baseball. He also played on the tennis team! He even appeared in the local newspaper, the *Pasadena Star-News*, in January 1937; it was reported that "for two years (Robinson) has been the outstanding athlete at Muir starring in football, basketball, track, baseball and tennis."

After graduating from John Muir, Jackie went to Pasadena Junior College (PJC) and continued dominating in his main four sports: football, track, baseball, and basketball. Throughout high school and junior college, Jackie played on nearly all-white teams and against nearly all-white teams too. He never saw it as a problem. He was the best player, so he should compete against other players who thought they were as good as he was; it didn't matter what color they were.

In 1938, Jackie was elected to the Junior College Baseball All-Southern Team. He was chosen as the Most Valuable Player (MVP) for the selected region. What is most amazing is that

Jackie himself said that baseball was his weakest sport among the four!

Towards the end of his time at PJC, Jackie's brother, Frank, died in a motorcycle accident. Jackie was trying to choose which university to attend and decided on the University of California, Los Angeles (UCLA) so that he could be near Frank's family to help them.

At UCLA he played quarterback on their football team, the Bruins. In 1939 they won their league with six wins, four ties, and no losses. In track, Jackie won the National Collegiate Athletic Association (NCAA) championship in long jump. He excelled at UCLA but had to leave before graduating to take a job and help his family.

HIS FIGHT FOR EQUALITY

After Pearl Harbor was bombed and the United States entered World War II, Jackie was drafted into the army. On July 6, 1944, while in the army and now an officer, Jackie got on an army bus. At the time, in the South where the army base was, buses were segregated. This meant that white passengers were seated at the front and black passengers at the back. This segregation was enforced by legislation known as the Jim Crow laws. The army, though, did not have segregated buses. However, when Jackie got on this bus, he was told by the driver to get to the back. He refused.

Eventually, the bus driver let him sit where he wanted, but when the bus came to a stop and Jackie got off, police were there to arrest him. At the station, Jackie stood up to the racist questioning from the investigating officer and he was recommended for a court-martial. A court-martial is a special court within the military. Jackie was likely to be kicked out of the army with a dishonorable discharge.

When the police approached Jackie's commander, Paul L. Bates of the 761st Battalion, and recommended that Jackie be court-martialed, Bates refused. Without the commander's agreement, the court-martial could not go ahead. To get around this, the army transferred Jackie to a different battalion. There the commander agreed to the court-martial. When the case came to trial, the jury of nine white officers found Jackie not guilty.

He went on to finish his time in the army and left with an honorable discharge. This was not the first, nor would it be the last time Jackie courageously stood up against racial injustice.

THE RIGHT MAN FOR THE JOB

After WWII, African Americans began to fight even more for equality, and this spilled over into baseball. A sign carried by a protester outside Yankee Stadium at the time read: "If we are able to stop bullets, why not balls?" By the 1940s, quite a few teams were looking for ways to bring black players into MLB.

Branch Ricky was the general manager for the MLB team the Brooklyn Dodgers. He wanted to recruit a black player into the Dodgers, but he was realistic. He needed a talented player, but he also knew he needed a player with a certain kind of character. He was aware of the abuse that the first black player would have to endure. He also knew that whoever it was would have to be able to take that abuse without fighting back and without getting angry. It was the only way that MLB would finally become open to everyone. It was going to take a very special person to be the first one to walk through that dangerous door.

At the time, Jackie was playing in the Negro League for a

team called the Kansas City Monarchs. He was not the best player in the Negro League, and many were not happy when Ricky chose him for the Dodgers. Ricky knew Jackie's talents, but more importantly, he knew his character. On August 28, 1945, they met before signing the contract. Ricky asked whether Jackie thought he could withstand the abuse fans and even other players would throw his way without fighting back. Jackie said he thought he could. To test him, for three hours Ricky called Jackie all of the horrible racist things he could think of, and Jackie remained calm. After that, Ricky knew for certain he had the right man for the job.

Later, Jackie said, "Plenty of times I wanted to haul off when somebody insulted me for the color of my skin, but I had to hold to myself. I knew I was kind of an experiment. The whole thing was bigger than me."

THE BEGINNING

Jackie started in the farm team for the Dodgers. Most Major League teams have a farm team where players play for a season or two. The managers then pick players to move to the Major League team. The Dodgers' farm team was the Montreal Royals.

In 1946, Jackie set off for spring training with the Royals in Florida. The problem was that Florida was a segregated state with Jim Crow laws. Because of this, Jackie couldn't sleep at the same hotel as his teammates or eat at the same restaurants. Throughout his baseball career, this would always be a problem for Jackie when they were in the South.

His first debut game with the Royals was against the Jersey City Giants. The catcher of the Giants ordered the pitcher, Warren Sandel, to throw the ball directly at Jackie when he was up to bat. Warren Sandel knew Jackie personally; they'd played baseball together in the past. He refused. This sort of rough, unsportsmanlike-like behavior was something Jackie faced with a lot of teams. As he had promised Ricky, he swallowed the abuse and played on. In that first game, he was up to bat five times and got four hits; he batted in three runs and stole two bases. It was clear he would not allow anything to get in his way to being successful.

The Royals struggled to get other teams to play with them. Some white players refused to play against a baseball team with a black player on it. Despite the abuse Jackie was having to stand up to, the fans in Montreal supported him. During that season, more than one million people attended the Royals' games. This was amazing and completely unheard of for a minor league farm team. They were there to watch Jackie play.

For the 1947 season, Jackie was called up to play for the Dodgers. His first official Major League in-season game was on April 15, 1947. At that debut game, there were 26,623 people in the stands, 14,000 of them black.

Some Dodgers players wanted to sit out the game. They didn't want to play with an African American. Manager Leo Durocher was not having it. He told them, "I do not care if the guy is yellow or black, or if he has stripes like a *** zebra. I'm the manager of this team and I say he plays." He threatened to have any player traded who refused to play with Jackie on the team.

Not all of his teammates were against Jackie, though. In one instance, when Jackie was being heckled by a racist fan, Pee Wee Reese, the captain of the Dodgers, left his position, walked over to Jackie, and put his arm around his shoulder as a sign of support for everyone to see. Later Pee Wee Reese said, "You can hate a man for many reasons. Color is not one of them."

Jackie and his family withstood constant abuse and even death threats, but he kept the promise he had made to Ricky and took it all with calm, courageous grace.

HIS BASEBALL CAREER

Jackie played professional baseball for ten seasons, all with the Brooklyn Dodgers. During that time, he played second base mostly, occasionally first. In 1947, his first year in the Majors, he won the Rookie of the Year Award for MLB. He played in six All-Star Games from 1949 to 1954. In 1949 he won the National League Most Valuable Player (MVP) award. In that year, his batting average was .342 and he stole 37 bases. He played in six World Series with the Dodgers, who won it in 1955. In 1962 he was inducted into the Baseball Hall of Fame.

In 1997, for the first time in the history of professional baseball, they retired Jackie's number, 42. In 2004, the day on which Jackie had played his first Major League baseball game, 15 April, was declared Jackie Robinson Day. Now, on that day, everyone in the entire Major League wears the number 42 in honor of Jackie Robinson, the man who was brave enough to cut the path for the African American players who came after him.

Jackie Robinson inspired many and still does. How he conducted himself and the risks he took made it easier for those who followed him inside and outside of baseball. Dr. Martin Luther King Jr said, "Jackie Robinson made my success possible. Without him, I would never have been able to do what I did."

DISCUSSION QUESTIONS

1. Why do you think Branch Ricky wanted Jackie Robinson to stay calm when faced with racist abuse?

2. What characteristics of Jackie's made him the best man for the job?

3. What were Jim Crow laws and how did they make Jackie's life more difficult?

FREE BONUS CONTENT

CHAPTER 3
LOU GEHRIG

"LOU GEHRIG WAS *a guy who could really hit the ball, was dependable and seemed so durable that many of us thought he could have played forever.*"

– George Selkirk, Gehrig's teammate

INTRODUCTION

Lou Gehrig played for the New York Yankees for the whole of his career. He's considered one of the best baseball players and best batters of all time, but when he played for the Yankees, he was overshadowed by his larger-than-life teammate, Babe Ruth. Babe, with his massive, outgoing personality, lived in the spotlight. He even batted first on the batting order, with Lou Gehrig batting second. Lou was a quiet, calm, consistent gentleman. He showed the world another way. He showed us that working hard and consistently showing up every day while doing your best can lead to greatness too.

A SON OF NEW YORK

Gehrig was born in New York City on June 19, 1903. His parents, Christina Fox and Heinrich Gehrig, were German immigrants. In fact, Gehrig didn't learn to speak English until he was five. Although his parents had four children, only Lou lived past childhood. Gehrig's mother worked as a maid and was the breadwinner of the family since his father was an epileptic and an alcoholic and was often unemployed.

Gehrig played baseball and football throughout his childhood. When he was seventeen, he traveled to Chicago with his school, the New York School of Commerce. They played at Wrigley Field against the local team, Lane Tech High School, in front of a crowd of 10,000.

At the bottom of the ninth inning, with Gehrig's team winning 8-6 and the bases loaded, he hit a home run that went out of the stadium. This was an incredible feat at the time. The young Gehrig got his first national attention that day.

He was a hardworking, intelligent boy. He finished high school and went on to study engineering at Columbia University on a football scholarship. While there, he became a member of the Phi Delta Theta fraternity.

John McGraw, the then manager of the New York Giants, advised the young Gehrig to not waste his summer off from university and instead to play professional baseball to earn some money and keep in shape. Gehrig was not sure about it since the rules for his scholarship stated that he could not play professional sports while at university. McGraw told him it wouldn't be a problem because he could play under a fake name. Gehrig was persuaded and played twelve professional games with the Giants as Henry Lewis. That fake name didn't work, though, because he was found out. He was suspended from playing university sports for a year but luckily didn't lose his scholarship.

In 1922, he was back to playing for Columbia. He was a star on both the football and baseball teams at the university. On April 18, 1923, Gehrig was pitching and struck out seventeen of the opponent's batters in a row, setting a record for Columbia. In the stands was a scout for the Yankees, Paul Krichell. Krichell was not as impressed by Gehrig's pitching as he was with his batting. He saw a powerful left-handed batter and knew he had to have Gehrig on the Yankees.

On April 29, 1923, Gehrig signed with the Yankees, joining the team mid-season. At first he was only playing as a pinch hitter, someone who stepped into the batting order for another player who was in the starting line-up. He didn't get a chance to start a game for a while, but when he did, he never let that chance go.

THAT LUCKY HEADACHE

That opportunity arrived on June 2, 1925, when the Yankees' first base player, Wally Pipp, had a headache. Someone needed to play first base, and that someone was Lou Gehrig. Later Pipp would remark, "I took the two most expensive aspirins." He said that because from that day until he retired, Lou Gehrig played first base for the Yankees without missing a single day. He set a baseball record that stood for 56 years. He played 2,130 consecutive games, meaning he never missed a single one. If the Yankees had a game during that time, Gehrig always played. That record was part of the reason that he was nicknamed The

Iron Horse. During that long stretch of games, there were many times Gehrig nearly had to give up and miss a game or two, but he never did. Yankee catcher Bill Dickey said about Gehrig, "He just went out and did his job every day."

One example of when Gehrig nearly had to give up was on April 23, 1933. During a league game, a pitched ball hit him in the head and he was nearly knocked unconscious. He managed to recover enough to finish the game. In another example, in an exhibition game the day before a league game, he was actually knocked out by a pitch that hit him above his right eye. He was unconscious for five minutes, but the next day he was back on the field playing. When he reached 1999 consecutive games, already 700 games ahead of the record at the time, his wife Eleanor begged him to take a sick day. He refused and played on.

What finally stopped his consecutive days of playing was the disease that would eventually kill him. During the 1938 season, Gehrig's performance was off. The doctors discovered that he had a rare disease of the nervous system called amyotrophic lateral sclerosis (ALS). (Later it would be renamed Lou Gehrig Disease.) He knew that the disease was threatening the performance of the Yankees, so he eventually took himself out of the game. He told Joe McCarthy, the manager of the Yankees, that he needed to retire. "I'm benching myself, Joe," he told the Yankees' manager on May 2, 1939. Gehrig was only 36 years old. It was a shock to everyone. The last game he played and the last in his amazing streak was on April 30, 1939.

Speaking at Lou Gehrig Day, McCarthy said about receiving that news, "Lou, what else can I say except that it was a sad day in the life of everybody who knew you when you came into my hotel room that day in Detroit and told me you were quitting as a ballplayer because you felt yourself a hindrance to the team. My God, man, you were never that."

LEGACY

Besides his record for consecutive days of play, Gehrig was an exceptional batter. He was the league's Most Valuable Player (MVP) twice, in 1927 and 1936. In the 1934 season, he hit the baseball Triple Crown. He had the highest batting average in the league, .363, the highest runs batted in at 165, and the highest number of home runs at 49. He played with the Yankees in seven World Series and won six. He played first base in the All-Star Games seven times, between 1933 and 1939, and he was the captain of the Yankees from 1935 to 1941.

He entered the Baseball Hall of Fame in 1939. In 1969, he was voted the best baseball player of all time by the Baseball Writers' Association of America, and he received the most votes in the MLB All-Century Team in 1999.

According to McCarthy, Gehrig "...was the finest example of a ballplayer, sportsman and citizen that baseball has ever known."

LOU GEHRIG DAY

On July 4, 1939, the Yankees celebrated Lou Gehrig Day. They were playing a double-header, and in between the two games, people from around the country, both in baseball and out, came to honor Gehrig.

On that day, Gehrig gave a speech that is often called The Gettysburg Address for Baseball. In it, though many felt he'd been given a bad hand by getting the disease that forced him to leave the game he loved, he told the gathering, "Today I consider myself the luckiest man on the face of the earth."

LOU GEHRIG MEMORIAL AWARD

In 1955, Gehrig's fraternity at Columbia University established an award in his honor named the Lou Gehrig Memorial Award. The award recognizes baseball players who have made an "exemplary contribution to both the community and to philanthropy." The first winner in 1955 was Alvin Dark, a player for the New York Giants. The second year it was Pee Wee Reese, the Dodgers' captain who stood with Jackie Robinson against the racists.

DEATH

Gehrig died on June 2, 1941, seventeen days before his 38th birthday. His wife never remarried. When asked why, years later, she said, "I had the best of it. I would not have traded two minutes of my life with that man for 40 years with another."

On the day he died, the mayor of New York City, Fiorello Henry La Guardia, ordered that all flags in the city fly at half-mast to honor Lou Gehrig, that much-loved son of New York City.

DISCUSSION QUESTIONS

1. What do you think about Lou Gehrig "benching" himself? Explain.

2. Lou Gehrig and Babe Ruth were both big hitters for the Yankees at the same time. How were they different?

3. Why do you think Wally Pipp said he took the two most expensive aspirins ever?

FREE BONUS CONTENT

CHAPTER 4
ROBERTO CLEMENTE

"ANY TIME *you have the opportunity to accomplish something for somebody who comes behind you and you do not do it, you are wasting your time on Earth.*"

— Roberto Clemente

INTRODUCTION

Roberto Clemente was an exceptional baseball player. He pulled up a struggling team, the Pittsburgh Pirates, from losing to being a star in the National League and eventual World Series winners twice. All he did for baseball is little compared to what he did for the world. Roberto Clemente was more than a baseball player; he was a humanitarian, a person who believed in service to the community. On his home island of Puerto Rico, he's a national hero. In 1964, when he married his wife, Vera, thousands of starry-eyed fans lined the streets to see the famous couple.

He was a devout Catholic his entire life, and because of his good works, some would like Roberto Clemente to be canonized by the Church; that means the Pope would make him a saint. Even without official sainthood, he was a saintly man who lived his life with integrity and compassion for others. His biographer, Kal Wagenheim, said that he "...believed passionately in the virtue and dignity of hard work ... that a man should revere his parents, wife and children, his country, and God. He believed just as fiercely in his personal worth and integrity."

These things together created a man who can inspire all of us.

EARLY LIFE

Roberto Enrique Clemente Walker was born on August 18, 1934, in Cardina, Puerto Rico. He was the youngest of seven children. His mother, Luisa Walker, would be an inspiration to him in his life. He claimed she had as good a throwing arm as he did. His father, Melchor Clemente, worked in the sugar industry. Clemente and his brothers often worked with their father in the sugar cane fields to bring in more income for the struggling family.

Clemente always loved baseball. One of his baseball idols was the African American player Monte Irvin. Irvin used to come to Puerto Rico in the off-season to play with the San Juan Senators, a team Clemente would later manage. Clemente and his friends would carry the players' bags so that they could get free entrance to the games. Monte could see the enthusiasm in young Clemente and gifted him a ball and glove.

Clemente was also good at track and field. At one point, he was an Olympic hopeful for Puerto Rico in high jump and javelin. Eventually, he gave both of them up to focus on baseball, but he credits his javelin throwing for his well-respected throwing arm in baseball. He learned the physics of throwing and how to position his body effectively from his training in javelin.

At seventeen, Clemente was playing professional baseball with the Santurce Crabbers, a team in the Puerto Rican Baseball League. He was spotted there and originally signed a contract with the Brooklyn Dodgers in 1954 when he was eighteen. Shortly after that signing, because of a rule in MLB, the Pittsburgh Pirates snatched Clemente from the Dodgers. He would go on to play eighteen seasons with Pittsburgh.

BASEBALL LEGEND

Clemente started with the Pirates on April 17, 1955, playing right field. His first few years in the Major League were not very good. He suffered from injuries, and his inability to speak English was a problem too.

Despite a lot of downtime, when Clemente did play he showed what he could do. On July 25, 1956, he performed a near miracle. The Pirates were playing the Cubs and losing. He hit something called a walk-off home run. This is a home run at the bottom of the final inning of the game that causes the batting team to win the game. In this case, Clemente got to bat when the bases were loaded and hit an in-field home run, meaning the ball did not leave the park but he and the three other players on bases made it home, scoring four runs and winning the game for the Pirates, 9-8. Such a feat had not yet happened in modern baseball.

Eventually, Clemente became one of the star players for the

Pirates, accomplishing extraordinary catches in right field and making his mark batting too. During his time with the Pirates, he won four National League batting titles, in 1966 he was chosen as the National League MVP, and he won twelve MLB Gold Glove Awards for exceptional fielding.

In 1960, the Pirates won the World Series against the Yankees in seven games. Clemente's batting average for the Series was .310. In 1971, they won the World Series again. His batting average for the Series that time was an incredible .414. He was chosen as the MVP for the Series. He made exactly 3000 hits in his professional career, one of only eleven players to have ever achieved that.

In 1972 when he died, he was at the top of his game. The following year, he was inducted into the Baseball Hall of Fame. He was the first Caribbean and Latin American player to be inducted.

FIGHTER FOR EQUALITY

In 1954, by the time Clemente joined MLB, the situation for non-white players was grim, despite Jackie Robinson having stepped onto the MLB field in 1947, seven years previously. In 1954, 90.7% of the players in MLB were white, 5.6% African American, and only 3.7% Latino. Clemente accepted the responsibility of representing Puerto Rico, the Caribbean, and Latin America in MLB. He also wanted equality for all non-white players. He took his role seriously to make things easier for those who would come after him.

Some sports commentators, as well as the makers of baseball cards, wanted to "Americanize" Clemente and started calling him Bob or Bobby instead of Roberto. Clemente stood against this, feeling that it was an insult to his Latin American heritage, which he was proud of. He insisted that they stop calling him by a name that was not his. There was no need to Americanize Hispanic names since those names were already American.

Spring training for the Pirates was in the South where Jim Crow laws were still in force. Clemente and the other non-white Pirates could not eat at the same restaurant as the white players did. The norm was for the non-white players to eat on the bus, the food being brought out to them from the restaurant where the white players were eating. Roberto would not have it. He told the other players on the bus that if they touched that food, they would have to answer to him. He said if they were not good enough to enter the restaurant and eat, then the food was not good enough to feed them. He would not allow them to be humiliated in that way. He insisted that they would not sleep in separate hotels either. He told the Pirates' management that they needed to solve that problem. In the end, they rented a large house where all of the team members could stay together to avoid the segregated hotels and restaurants.

Puerto Rico is part of the United States, but Clemente didn't like that Puerto Ricans were not treated like other Americans. "I am an American citizen ... [but] to people here, we are foreigners, outsiders," he said. He also continually complained that black and Hispanic players didn't get the same recognition as white players. Management across the MLB was all white, and he said that situation needed to change. He said non-white players should be given equal sponsorships and endorsements too. Whenever he had a chance when speaking, he pushed for the equality of non-white players in baseball.

HUMANITARIAN

Clemente believed that a life was given to a person so that they could be of service to their fellow humans. Pirates general manager Joe Brown once said, "I don't think Clemente turned down many people who wanted his help – if anybody."

During off seasons, Clemente went to Puerto Rico where he held baseball clinics for kids. He worked on various humanitarian causes around Latin America, often organizing donations of food and baseball equipment.

In 1970, the Pirates declared 24 July Roberto Clemente Day to honor all that he had done for the team. Clemente wouldn't agree to the day unless it included fundraising for the Pittsburgh Children's Hospital. He asked fans to make donations to the hospital in his name on the day. They raised $5,500, which was used to help poor parents pay for their children's medical expenses. Even on the road, he visited hospitals to see sick fans and sign autographs.

THE NICARAGUAN EARTHQUAKE

At 12:29 a.m. on December 23, 1972, an earthquake of magnitude 6.3 hit Managua, Nicaragua. It devastated the country. Between 4000 and 11,000 people died, and 20,000 were injured. Clemente had just been to Nicaragua as part of the Amateur World Series from November 15 to December 5. When the earthquake hit, Clemente was devastated. The people of Nicaragua had been so wonderful to him, and he couldn't ignore them when they needed his help.

He immediately began organizing donations for Nicaragua. His wife said during the entire festive period that year he barely slept or ate; he didn't even open the Christmas presents he'd received. He was too busy organizing help for the Nicaraguans. He even went door to door in the rich neighborhoods or barrios in Puerto Rico asking for money. He raised $150,000 and 26 tons of food.

He sent the first shipments of aid to Nicaragua on three flights, but it was stolen by corrupt officials in the Nicaraguan government. Clemente decided he would accompany the aid on the fourth flight so he could make sure it got to the people who needed it.

He planned the fourth trip for New Year's Eve. Unfortunately, the plane he chartered was not in the best condition, and because of the holiday, it didn't have all the staff it required. There was no flight engineer or co-pilot on the plane. To make things worse, the plane was overloaded by 4200 pounds.

Soon after take-off, at 9:23 pm, the plane crashed into the Atlantic Ocean off the coast of Puerto Rico, killing all five passengers, including Clemente. His body was never found.

LEGACY

The world was shocked by Clemente's death while in service to others. The US president at the time, President Nixon, said, "He sacrificed his life on a mission of mercy." Later in 1973, Nixon invited Vera to the White House to receive the Congressional Medal of Honor on behalf of her husband. In 2003, President George W. Bush invited Vera to the White House again to accept the Medal of Freedom for Roberto Clemente.

Vera and her sons, Roberto Jr, Luis, and Enrique, went on to set up the Clemente Foundation, which is still doing humanitarian work in Clemente's name.

Clemente was a talented, exceptional baseball player, but he viewed his success on the field as part and parcel of his call to service. His life and even his death should inspire us to find areas in our own lives where we can serve others too.

DISCUSSION QUESTIONS

1. Give two instances where Clemente showed that he was a humanitarian.

2. How would you feel if your teammates ate their meals in a restaurant but you had to eat in the bus?

3. What is integrity? Give an example of when Clemente showed integrity.

FREE BONUS CONTENT

CHAPTER 5
JULIE CROTEAU

"THERE'S *no reason why baseball can't be co-ed. It's not that women aren't interested in baseball. It's just not having a chance."*

— Julie Croteau

INTRODUCTION

Julie Croteau had a passion for baseball from the time that she was a little girl. She played tee-ball when she was very small. That's a sort of baseball where the ball is not pitched but rather sits on a stand or tee and swung at. Then she played Little League with a batting average of .300. She loved baseball and was good at it and never considered the possibility that she would be denied the chance to play it once she reached high school. But she was. Despite being as good a player as any of the boys on her team, she was advised to go and play softball with the girls. The thing was she didn't want to play softball, she wanted to play baseball, and she didn't see any reason why she shouldn't. Her fight to play baseball would begin to open the path for women to play in MLB, but only begin.

A DREAM DENIED

Julie Croteau was born on December 4, 1970, in Prince William County, Virginia. Both of her parents were lawyers. Croteau loved baseball from the beginning. She was an average batter but an excellent first-base player.

When she started high school at Osbourn Park High School, she tried out for the all-male baseball team, the Yellow Jackets. The team's coach called her parents and suggested that she would be more comfortable playing softball with the girls. On February 20, 1988, Croteau ignored the coach's phone call and tried out for his baseball team. She was a baseball player, not a softball player. She was good, good enough to be chosen for the team, but soon afterward she was cut. Croteau knew that she was cut only because she was a girl, and she knew that was unfair.

TO COURT THEY GO

Croteau and her parents decided to take the school to court. There is a law called Title IX which says that any school that gets funding from the federal government, which is most schools, cannot stop girls from playing any of the sports that the school offers. They cannot discriminate because of gender. Croteau and her parents thought what the baseball coach did was in violation of Title IX.

The court heard the case on March 28, 1988. Twelve of the seventeen boys on the school baseball team were in court to support the coach. The five who couldn't come to the court wrote letters supporting the coach's decision to keep Croteau off the team. They said that the team was made up of the best seventeen players at the school. Croteau was just not good enough. It didn't seem that they were the best seventeen players because the Yellow Jackets had a record of only 4 wins, 13 losses, and one tie.

The trial made national news, and reporters interviewed many people about the sort of baseball player Croteau was. Her coach from Big League (the league children play in after Little League from the ages of 16 to 18) said, "She's a young lady with a lot of heart and fortitude and the skills to go along with it."

One of the coaches from the Catholic University where Croteau attended some baseball clinics said, "I think she's just as capable of playing first base as many of the boys. She has average high school ability for boys. She's a line drive hitter, and she makes good contact. I'm seeing seventy to eighty high school games a year, and she has enough ability to make most high school teams."

Despite these glowing comments that showed she had the skill to play baseball on the high school team with the boys, Croteau lost the case. The judge said she "...received a fair try out and that the decision to cut her was made in good faith and for reasons unrelated to gender." Croteau was crushed by the court's ruling. "I remember when I left the courthouse and I was really upset because I didn't feel like justice had been served," she said.

Mike Zitz was a reporter who attended the trial. When the

decision was read out by the judge, he watched the boys from the baseball team jump up and shout with happiness. Zitz could see that the trial had been a blow to Croteau. Besides being a reporter, he was also the manager for the Fredericksburg Giants, a semi-professional male team in the Virginia Baseball League. He asked Croteau to try out for the team. She ended up making the team and played for them for several seasons.

COLLEGE BASEBALL

St. Mary's College in Maryland heard about the trial and contacted Croteau. They told her that if she came to their college and tried out and got chosen for the boys' baseball team, no one would stop her from playing. So she set off for St Mary's after graduating from high school. In 1989, as a freshman, she made the team and was now the first base player for the St Mary's Seahawks. She was the first woman to play, and to play regularly, on a men's National Collegiate Athletics Association (NCAA) college baseball team. She was making history.

Croteau and her entire team were very nervous their first game because eleven national news outlets were there to cover the game, including NBC and CNN. The game was played against Spring Garden College from Philadelphia. The Seahawks lost 4-1. Though Croteau was up to bat three times and didn't get a hit, she didn't strike out either. At first base, she fielded six balls perfectly. She proved that she was as good as any of the men on the team. The coach for Spring Garden College, Jack Bilbee, said of Croteau's performance in that first game, "I thought she was one of their better players. Especially with two strikes on her. She really hung in there."

Though at first Croteau felt supported at St Mary's by most

of the people there, things changed. "What happened is that for some reason I was this hero and everyone accepted it and the media covered it and the media and school were telling everyone it was a great thing, let's not destroy it. So everyone believed it.... When the media went away, so did the message," Croteau said. She was harassed and bullied by teammates and members of the athletic department until, in her junior year, she quit the team and took a leave of absence from the college.

The summer of 1992, though, she was back playing for Mike Zitz's Giants.

PLAYING PROFESSIONAL BASEBALL

In 1994, Croteau made it onto a semi-professional women's baseball team, the Colorado Silver Bullets. Though it was a women's team, they traveled the country playing against semi-professional and minor league men's teams. When playing for the Silver Bullets, Croteau's fielding percentage, meaning the time a ball came to her on first base divided into the times she successfully finished the play was .989, near perfect.

The winter of 1994, Croteau and her Silver Bullet teammate Lee Ann Ketcham played baseball on the male baseball team the Maui Stingrays. This team was part of the Hawaii Winter Baseball League, a league affiliated with MLB. The two were the first women to play in an MLB-sanctioned league.

COACHING BASEBALL

In 1993, Croteau coached NCAA baseball at Western New England University as an assistant, and from 1995 to 1996, she was an assistant coach at the University of Massachusetts Amherst.

In 2004, she was asked to be the third-base coach for the US Women's National Baseball Team at the World Cup in Taiwan. They won a gold medal. She was the first woman to manage a women's baseball team to gold in an international competition.

Croteau was honored for her contribution to baseball when the National Baseball Hall of Fame Museum in Cooperstown, New York, made her glove from her time playing first base at St Mary's a permanent exhibit.

Reflecting on her time playing baseball, Croteau said she often had to be careful about how she did things as she was not only playing as herself; she was representing all girls and women who wanted to play baseball. She seemed to have been born with her passion for the game, but her passion for social justice was learned along the way as she saw what women faced in sport.

Even now, girls are allowed to play baseball with boys only until they reach high school. Once there, the girls are shut out. This is why they don't get baseball scholarships to colleges. When MLB teams are looking for new players, they look for them on college baseball teams. Since the women players are excluded at high school, MLB has only male players to choose from. As long as this situation remains, women will be shut out of MLB. Croteau had some success and opened a few doors for women, but there is still a long way to go in the battle for equality and justice for women in baseball.

DISCUSSION QUESTIONS

1. Do you think it was a good idea for Julie Croteau to take her high school to court, even though she lost? Why or why not?

2. Why do you think Croteau quit baseball at St. Mary's after her junior year?

3. What is discrimination? Do you think Croteau faced discrimination because of her gender? Why or why not?

FREE BONUS CONTENT

CHAPTER 6
HENRY "HANK" AARON

"Throughout the past century, the home run has held a special place in baseball and I have been privileged to hold this record for 33 of those years. I move over now and offer my best wishes to Barry and his family on this historical achievement. My hope today, as it was on that April evening in 1974, is that the achievement of this record will inspire others to chase their own dreams."
– Henry "Hank" Aaron (speaking when Barry Bond was about to break his record)

INTRODUCTION

IN 2002, when Henry Aaron was at the White House to receive the highest honor for a civilian in the United States, the Presidential Medal of Freedom, President George W. Bush said of Aaron, "By steadily pursuing his calling in the face of unreasoning hatred, Hank Aaron has proven himself a great human being as well as a great athlete."

It's difficult to be exceptional. And difficult to beat a long-standing record like the record for home runs that Babe Ruth held. But it's even harder to do that when everywhere you go people are pouring hate on you, some even hoping you'll die. Henry "Hank" Aaron put his head down and kept on his path, up against so many people who wanted to see him fail. In the end, despite what he was facing, he succeeded.

EARLY DAYS IN BASEBALL

Henry Aaron was born in Mobile, Alabama, on February 5, 1934. His family was poor and he didn't have baseball equipment. He and the other kids used to hit bottle caps with sticks. Sometimes they made bats and balls from anything they found around. From a young age, his hero was Jackie Robinson. In March 1948, Jackie Robinson was playing in Mobile, and young Aaron went to hear him speak. He became inspired when Robinson spoke about how things in the country were changing for African Americans. It pushed Aaron to dream big.

His high school in Mobile didn't have a baseball team, so Aaron tried out for the semi-professional Mobile Black Bears, an independent black team. He made it onto the team. He also played for the Pritchard Athletics, another independent black team. When he was 15 years old, he tried out for the Brooklyn Dodgers but didn't get a place.

In November 1951, he started playing for the Indianapolis Clowns, a team in the Negro American League. It was when traveling around with the Clowns that he got to see the viciousness of racism around the United States. He lived in the South and was used to the racist Jim Crow laws, but he thought in the North things would be different. Sadly, they were not.

In one of the many instances, the team was eating dinner at a restaurant in Washington D.C. Aaron said that as the restaurant's staff took the plates back to the kitchen after the team had eaten, the team could hear the plates being broken and thrown away. The restaurant threw the plates away because black men had eaten from them. Aaron would deal with such racism his entire baseball career. He didn't hide that it affected his feelings about playing baseball.

He didn't play long for the Clowns because word got out about how talented he was. After a handful of months, he received telegrams from both the New York Giants and the Braves, which were, at the time, in Boston. They would later move to Milwaukee, then finally to Atlanta. Both the Braves and the Giants wanted Aaron on their team. At the Clowns, he'd already built up an impressive record, with a batting average of .366, five home runs, 36 runs batted in, and 41 hits, and he'd only played 26 games! Now he had the chance to join MLB.

The Braves contract offered him $50 more, so he chose them over the Giants. He signed with them on June 12, 1952. The Braves bought his contract from the Clowns. The general manager of the Braves paid $10,000 to the Clowns for Aaron, but even then, when the height of his talent had not been revealed, he said Aaron was worth $100,000. Aaron started playing baseball with the Braves' minor league farm teams.

In 1952 he played for the Eau Claire Bears in Wisconsin. He played 87 games and got 116 hits, 61 runs batted in, and nine home runs. He was voted Rookie of the Year for that league.

Though he was excelling on the field, he was near heart-broken off it. He was homesick and struggling with constant racism in a league where nearly everyone was white, including the fans. He wanted to quit. His brother Herbert told him he was unlikely to get another opportunity like the one he had and advised him to try to find a way to stay. Aaron did.

He played the 1953 season with another one of the Braves' farm teams. They won the championship for the league, and he was voted MVP. One sports writer wrote, "Henry Aaron led the league in everything except hotel accommodation."

Aaron spent the 1953 off-season in Puerto Rico. There a few things changed. He got important coaching advice from another player, Mickey Owen. Aaron had been playing shortstop or second base but was not very good at in-field positions. Owen thought he'd be better in the outfield and helped him make the move to right field. He also taught Aaron how to hold the bat correctly so that he now had more control over where he sent the balls that he hit.

In the 1954 season, Aaron finally moved to the major league for the Braves.

A STAR BATTER

From his first game with the Braves, Aaron showed he would be a star batter. He didn't have the normal physique of a power hitter, being quite lightweight, but he had good forearms and wrists and used them to hit balls over the back wall regularly. Beyond that, he was a keen student of pitchers. Before a game, he studied the pitcher he would face. Even from the dugout, his eyes were glued to the pitcher's mound. He knew what to expect from the pitcher he was up against when he stepped into the batter's box.

On September 23, 1957, Aaron did something incredible. They were playing the St. Louis Cardinals in Milwaukee. It was the bottom of the last inning and the Braves were losing – and to make matters worse, they were playing for the National League pennant and a chance to play in the World Series. Aaron got up to bat with one person on base and hit a home run. The Braves won the pennant. It was the only walk-off home run to have ever won a team the pennant in the history of MLB.

The Braves went on the win the World Series against the New York Yankees. Aaron had a fantastic World Series, with a batting average of .393, three home runs, and seven runs batted in. In that year, he was chosen as the National League's Most Valuable Player.

He would continue to hit home run after home run, racking up an impressive total until someone noticed that he was getting near to breaking Babe Ruth's record of 714 home runs in his career.

BEATING THE BABE

Aaron had a different opinion about baseball records. He thought a player should play to the best of his ability; records were not so important. The media and baseball followers thought otherwise. At the end of the 1972 season, Aaron's career home run total stood at 672. The idea that Aaron might break Babe Ruth's record of 714 became a national obsession.

Some people encouraged him and were happy that he was likely to break the record. Other people, though, didn't want Babe Ruth's record broken by anyone, especially a black man. Aaron began to receive racist hate mail and death threats. He was by then a married man with children. They also received death threats.

During the 1973 season, Aaron's home run total kept increasing. The last game that season, in which Aaron hit a home run, was on September 29, 1973. His total at the end of the season was 713 home runs. It was nearly certain that in the first few days of the 1974 baseball season, Aaron would match Babe Ruth's record and then overtake it. During that off-season, his life was in even more danger. Even people who supported him got death threats and racist hate mail that year.

The executive sports editor at *The Atlanta Journal*, Lewis Grizzard, felt the threat that Aaron would not live to see the 1974 season was so high that he quietly prepared his obituary for the newspaper. Aaron was deeply hurt when some of the fans in Atlanta also hurled hate his way. In his memoir, Aaron wrote, "I didn't expect the fans to give me a standing ovation every time I stepped on the field, but I thought a few of them might come over to my side as I approached Ruth. At the very least, I felt I had earned the right not to be verbally abused and racially ravaged in my home ballpark."

Babe Ruth's widow, Claire Hodgson, was upset by the racial hatred Aaron experienced. She spoke publicly, saying that she knew that Babe would have supported Aaron and would have enthusiastically cheered him on to overtake the record. "I never wanted them to forget Babe Ruth. I just wanted them to remember Henry Aaron," Aaron said.

That year, the US postal service gave him a plaque because he was the person (excluding politicians) who had received the most pieces of mail that year – 930,000. The Braves even hired someone to take care of all of Aaron's mail. Quite a bit of it was hate mail.

THE RECORD FALLS

The first games for the Braves in the 1974 season were three games played in Cincinnati against the Reds. The Braves knew that if Aaron played, he'd like a tie and even to break the record at another team's stadium. They wanted the historic event to happen in Atlanta. They decided they would bench Aaron for those first three away games. The baseball commissioner, Bowie Kuhn, decided they could not. Aaron had to play in at least two of those games.

On Thursday, April 4, 1974, up against the Red's pitcher, Jack Billingham, Aaron hit a home run and tied Babe Ruth's record of 714 career home runs.

On that next Monday, April 8, 1974, in Atlanta, in front of a record crowd of 53,775, Aaron stepped into the batter's box. Al Downing was pitching for the Dodgers. The first pitch was a ball and Aaron let it pass. The second pitch, Aaron swung and hit his 715th home run and beat the record! He received an 11-minute standing ovation.

The broadcaster for the Dodgers, Vin Scully, could not contain his emotions. At the time, he said, "What a marvelous moment for baseball; what a marvelous moment for Atlanta and the state of Georgia; what a marvelous moment for the country and the world. A black man is getting a standing ovation in the Deep South for breaking a record of an all-time baseball idol. And it is a great moment for all of us, and particularly for Henry Aaron... And for the first time in a long time, that poker face of Aaron shows the tremendous strain and relief of what it must have been like to live with for the past several months."

Aaron hit the last home run of his career on June 20, 1976, in Milwaukee and ended with a career total of 755 home runs. He retired and went into baseball management with the Braves and into various corporate positions. He was inducted into the Baseball Hall of Fame on August 1, 1982. He died quietly in his sleep at his home in Atlanta on January 22, 2021, at the age of 86. The governor of Georgia ordered the flags in the state to fly at half-mast. Five US presidents paid tribute to Aaron: Joe Biden, Jimmy Carter, Bill Clinton, George W. Bush, and Barack Obama.

DISCUSSION QUESTIONS

1. How would you feel if you were Hank Aaron in Washington DC when the restaurant broke the plate you just ate from?

2. Hank Aaron didn't care much about breaking records. Other people cared a lot about breaking records. What do you think is important?

3. Why did Lewis Grizzard decide to write Hank Aaron's obituary in 1974, long before he died?

FREE BONUS CONTENT

CHAPTER 7
SANDY KOUFAX

"Sandy is a warm, friendly, honest, intelligent human being, one of the finest human beings I have ever known, but the truth is he was never very colorful."
— Buzzie Bavasi

INTRODUCTION

FOR SOME, the quiet, dignified Sandy Koufax was the best pitcher that ever played the game of baseball. Surprisingly, his first years in the major league went so badly that he was ready to quit and take up work at an electronics company he'd invested in. Thankfully, he decided to give it one more season, a season that changed everything. Along his not-so-perfect path, and despite his quiet way, when things mattered to him, he stood his ground. He stood for things he believed in and showed the world that integrity and commitment to your beliefs matter.

EARLY LIFE

Sandy Koufax (born Sandford Braun) was born on December 30, 1935, in Brooklyn, New York. His parents divorced when he was three. For the next six years, his mother, an accountant, worked, and he was raised mostly by his grandmother. When he was nine, his mother met and married Irving Koufax, an attorney, and Sandy took his stepfather's name.

He didn't start as a baseball player, though. He played basketball and even got a partial university scholarship for basketball. He had played some baseball when he was younger, but he caught people's attention when he played at the University of Cincinnati where he was studying architecture. There he played baseball in the spring of his first year. He pitched only 32 innings but threw 51 strikeouts. Suddenly, people were paying attention to his baseball playing, not his basketball.

Baseball scouts looking for new talent for their major league teams came to have a look at this 19-year-old pitcher. The scout for the Dodgers, Al Campanis, couldn't believe what he saw. "There are two times in my life the hair on my arms has stood up: The first time I saw the ceiling of theSistine Chapel and the second time, I saw Sandy Koufax throw a fastball."

Though eventually Koufax would sign with the Dodgers, his first major league try-out was with the New York Giants. He was invited to show them how he pitched. Koufax was so nervous at the try-out he pitched the ball wildly over the catcher's head. Eventually, though. Koufax got offers from the Dodgers, Pirates, Browns, and Giants. He decided, on the advice of his stepfather, to go with the Dodgers.

Buzzie Bavasi, the general manager for the Dodgers, remembered when Koufax and his stepfather, Irving Koufax, came to his office to negotiate the contract. Koufax wanted a $14,000 signing bonus and otherwise a standard contract. He thought if baseball didn't work out, he could use the $14,000 for fees to finish his degree in architecture. They agreed to a deal though the contract was not ready. They sealed it with a handshake.

Bavasi said he learned what kind of man Koufax was and what sort of family he came from on that day. As they were leaving Bavasi's office, Ed McCormick, a scout for the Giants, saw them. He knew what was up and quickly called his boss, telling him that they were about to lose Sandy Koufax to the Dodgers. His boss told him to offer Koufax $5000 more than what the Dodgers had offered. He did, and Koufax said no. He had an agreement with the Dodgers. Later, Bavasi said another family might have taken the money since the contract had not been signed, but not Koufax.

Everyone could see Koufax's talent as a pitcher, but it was raw talent. He had not played very much baseball and was inexperienced. In his first years at the Dodgers, that inexperience showed.

FAILING

In 1955, when Koufax joined the Dodgers, MLB had a rule called the Bonus Rule, which said that if a major league team signed a contract with a player that had a bonus of more than $4000, that player had to be on their list of 25 players that made up their team and the player had to be active in games. This presented a problem for the Dodgers. They had a 19-year-old Koufax who knew nearly nothing about fielding as a pitcher, or how to stop players from stealing bases, and knew only two signals the catcher gave the pitcher: one finger, meaning he should throw a fast ball, and two fingers, which meant he should throw a curve ball. There were six signals in all, but when the catcher gave Koufax any of the others, Koufax didn't know what he was talking about.

Normally, an inexperienced player such as Koufax would play in the minor farm teams for the Dodgers so that they would get the training they needed to play in the majors. Because of the Bonus Rule, the Dodgers had to put Koufax on the team. This meant pushing good, experienced players back to the minors to make space or trading them to other teams. It also meant that in 1955, when Koufax started playing the season for the Dodgers, it was a bit of a disaster.

The problem with Koufax was that he swung from being very good to being terrible, sometimes from one pitch to the next. Often, when a batter got a hit off his pitch, he would get nervous and emotional. He dealt with those feelings by throwing the next pitch even faster, but his fastest balls were also his wildest, with no control at all.

Every once in a while, though, Koufax showed brilliance. During a game on August 27, 1955, he struck out 14 batters in a single game, the most for any pitcher in the National League that season. The other team got only two hits off his pitches.

Since the Dodgers could never be sure what sort of pitching Koufax would produce on any day, he rarely started games, and even when he played, it was often for only a handful of innings. This went on for a few seasons. In 1960, Koufax was so frustrated with not getting the chance to play, he asked the Dodgers to trade him to another team. They refused.

After he played the last game of the 1960 season, he threw his gloves and spikes in the garbage, certain he was done with baseball for good. The clubhouse manager later fished them out and kept them in case Koufax decided to return.

A CHANGE OF HEART

While he was off before the 1961 season, Koufax decided that he would give baseball one more chance. If nothing improved, he would quit for good and go and work at the electronics business he'd invested in. For the first time in his life, he started training. He began to run daily and work out. "I decided I was really going to find out how good I can be," Koufax said.

In the 1961 season, everything changed. When the season ended, Koufax had broken the record for MLB for the number of career strikeouts with 269, and he'd done it in far fewer innings than the previous record holder, in fact, 110 innings less.

He now had much better control over his pitches, and the Dodgers' management saw it. He started 35 games that season and pitched 255.2 innings. It was the first year that he was voted into the All-Stars Game, too.

On April 19, 1963, he pitched his second immaculate inning. What that means is that three players from the other team got up to bat. Koufax threw three pitches for each batter and all were strikes. In all, only nine pitches were thrown for the inning; the other team had three outs and it was over. That feat was the first time any pitcher in the National League pitched two immaculate innings and only the second time in the history of MLB.

From then on, Koufax's performance only improved.

In 1963, from July 3 to July 16, Koufax pitched 33 consecutive scoreless innings. Included in that time were three shutouts, meaning there was not a single hit for the other team off

Koufax's pitches. That season, he was named the National League MVP.

In 1964, to the world's amazement, Koufax pitched yet another immaculate inning. He was the first player in MLB to have ever accomplished that. Unfortunately, that same season, during a game he suddenly felt his left arm, his pitching arm, "let go."

PITCHING WITH PAIN

From that moment early in the 1964 season, Koufax began to have problems with his pitching arm. The doctors dealt with the pain by giving him cortisone shots and after the game putting his elbow in ice. The team stopped having him pitch so many games in a row. Sometimes Koufax would wake up the day after pitching a game and his elbow would be the size of his knee. Other times he couldn't straighten his arm. Something was seriously wrong. The doctors told him that he had traumatic arthritis. They warned him if he kept pitching as he had been, when he was older, he could lose the complete use of his arm. He was only 29 years old.

Still, after resting during the off season, he started the 1965 season. The team doctors, and Koufax himself, learned to manage the disease. Despite the diagnosis, he excelled on the pitcher's mound.

On September 6, 1965, Koufax pitched a no-hitter. He was the sixth pitcher in modern baseball history to have done that. That season, the Dodgers won the National League pennant and were heading to the World Series.

A CLASH BETWEEN BASEBALL AND RELIGION

Game 1 for the World Series of 1965 fell on October 6, which was also Yom Kippur, the most important holy day for Jewish people. Sandy Koufax was Jewish, and he told the Dodgers' management that he would not be able to play the first game of the World Series because of his religion. This made their opponents, the Minnesota Twins, very happy. It also made Jewish Americans happy as it showed that Koufax valued his religion.

In Koufax's place, the Dodgers' other pitcher, Don Drysdale, stood in. In the third inning, something went wrong, and Drysdale allowed the Twins to make six home runs. The first game ended with the Dodgers losing 8-2. After the game, Drysdale joked with the team manager, Walter Alston, saying he thought Alston was probably wishing, after his poor performance, that he'd been Jewish too and sat out the game.

Once Koufax was back pitching, things started improving. In Game 5, Koufax pitched and they won 7-0, the Twins not able to get a single run off his pitching. The Dodgers won the World Series, and Koufax was chosen as the World Series MVP.

1966 HOLDOUT

Before 1966, baseball players were at the mercy of team owners and management when it came to pay. It was often a "take it or leave it" sort of situation. In 1966, Koufax and his pitching friend, Drysdale, showed players that it could be another way.

Both of the pitchers' contracts were up and they each began negotiations with management alone. When Koufax and Drysdale discussed what was going on, they realized that management was trying to use them against each other in an attempt to pay them less. Koufax saw this as unfair. They decided that they would instead negotiate together.

They approached management and asked that they be given $1 million for three years, $500,000 each. That was unheard of! The management refused. They offered them $30,000 per season. Koufax and Drysdale said no.

They decided they would hold out until they got what they wanted. When spring training started in 1966, the pitchers didn't show up. Management became very worried when spring training was over, the season was about to start, and the Dodgers were short two important pitchers.

Eventually, after much negotiation, they settled after 32 days. Koufax would get $125,000 and Drysdale would get $110,000 for the 1966 season. Koufax got a pay increase of $40,000 and Drysdale $30,000. It made Koufax the highest-paid player in MLB.

Later, when Marvin Miller, the first director of the baseball players' union, the Major League Baseball Player Association, was arguing for collective negotiation, he referred to the 1966 holdout by Koufax and Drysdale and how their working together in their negotiations led to a better deal for both of them.

RETIREMENT

After the 1966 season ended, Koufax surprised everyone by announcing that he would retire. He was 30 years old at the time and at the top of his game, but he wanted to make sure that he could still have the use of his arm after baseball. It was time to go. He said, "I've got a lot of years to live after baseball and I would like to live them with the complete use of my body. I don't regret one minute of the last twelve years, but I think I would regret one year that was too many."

He went on to have a very active retirement. In 1972, he was the youngest player ever to be inducted into the Baseball Hall of Fame.

Sandy Koufax played major league baseball for a short twelve years, and part of the time he was still learning the game, yet he broke records and accomplished things pitchers with much longer careers never could. He believed in hard work and integrity. These proved to be excellent guides.

DISCUSSION QUESTIONS

1. How did Koufax deal with such public failure? What do you think about that?

2. In 1966, Koufax thought management was dealing with him and Drysdale unfairly. Why?

3. Koufax refused to play Game 1 of the World Series because of his religion. What do you think about this?

FREE BONUS CONTENT

AFTERWORD

In this book, you met seven extraordinary baseball players. Players like Jackie Robinson, who stepped forward courageously to be the first African American in the major leagues in modern times. And Roberto Clemente who used his fame to show compassion for others. And then there's Babe Ruth who, when young, looked bound to be a failure, but by his own strength of mind, decided otherwise. You also met Julie Croteau, who continued playing baseball even when her own teammates didn't want her there because she believed that girls and women should be able to play baseball too. Then there was Hank Aaron who continued even when people wanted to kill him and his family. These are stories of bravery. In this book, you met brave, inspirational heroes.

But what is a hero? Yes, these players had talent in baseball, but many players do and not all inspire us. What sets these seven apart from the others?

Each had a set of values, and those values guided them in their life. They were willing to suffer to keep their values because they were so important to them. They were willing to do dangerous things, to be scared and still walk forward, to stay on their path even when it was hard and they wanted to stop.

So what is a hero?

A hero is an ordinary person who decides that what they value is so important that they will continue no matter what. They have characteristics such as ambition, persistence, integrity, dedication, and compassion. Those characteristics make their values. Any one of us could be a hero; there is not much difference between them and us. You might already be inspiring people around you.

Let these seven baseball legends inspire you to find the hero inside yourself!

THANK YOU!

Thank you so much for choosing my book among the many out there. It means a lot that you decided to dive into the world of baseball legends with me.

A BIG THANK YOU for not only picking up this book but also for sticking with it to the very end. Your journey through these pages is much appreciated.

PLEASE LEAVE A REVIEW

Before you close the final chapter, I have a small request. Would you mind leaving a review on the platform where you got this book? Your thoughts and opinions are incredibly valuable, especially for an independent author like myself. Sharing a review is a simple yet powerful way to support my work and help others discover these inspirational baseball stories.

Your feedback is crucial. It guides me in crafting books that resonate with you and provide the insights and enjoyment you seek. Hearing your thoughts would be truly meaningful to me.

Once again, thank you for being part of this baseball adventure!

ABOUT THE AUTHOR

SPORTS ENTHUSIAST TURNED AUTHOR, I've dedicated my life to inspiring young minds through captivating tales rooted in human perseverance and the wonders of imagination. With a background in education, I've witnessed the transformative power of storytelling in shaping resilient and inquisitive individuals.

My writings dive deep into the world of sports, revealing life lessons hidden within each moment of action. Beyond mere stories, I weave narratives filled with action, heart, and timeless teachings. To every teacher, parent, and young reader who has joined me on this journey: your passion fuels my tales.

Here's to more adventures and the boundless joy of discovery!

Forever grateful,
Emma

Made in the USA
Las Vegas, NV
26 November 2024

12744686R00046